BODY TALK
SOUND AND VISION
THE SENSORY SYSTEMS

JENNY BRYAN

Dillon Press
New York

BODY TALK

BREATHING

DIGESTION

MIND AND MATTER

MOVEMENT

REPRODUCTION

SMELL, TASTE AND TOUCH

SOUND AND VISION

THE PULSE OF LIFE

First Dillon Press Edition 1994

Dillon Press
Macmillan Publishing Company
866 Third Avenue
New York, NY 10022

Macmillan Publishing Company is part of the Maxwell
Communication Group of Companies.

First published in 1993 by Wayland (Publishers) Limited
61 Western Road, Hove, East Sussex, England BN3 1JD

Library of Congress Cataloging-in-Publication Data

Bryan, Jenny,
    Sound and vision : the sensory systems/Jenny Bryan.—1st Dillon
Press ed.
    p. cm. — (Body talk)
    Includes bibliographical references and index.
    ISBN: 0-87518-591-6
    1. Hearing—Juvenile literature. 2. Vision—Juvenile literature.
[1. Hearing. 2. Vision.] I. Title. II. Series.
QP462.2.B79 1994
612.8'4—dc20   93-37306

Summary: Describes the senses of sight and hearing and explores the
many ways these senses affect our lives.

Printed by G. Canale & C.S.p.A., Turin, Italy

1 2 3 4 5 6 7 8 9 10

CONTENTS

INTRODUCTION

Over millions of years, the eyes and ears of all living creatures have adapted to suit their needs for survival. Have you noticed that a cat's eyes shine in the dark? Cats have a special membrane over their eyes that reflects light so they can see to hunt at night. An African serval cat has huge swiveling ears that are almost as large as its head. In fact, its ears are so sensitive that a serval can hear the telltale sound of a mouse nibbling in the grass.

Look at a rabbit's eyes. They are on the sides of its head, not the front. A rabbit needs to be able to see all around in case a fox or another of its enemies is about to attack. Having eyes so far apart gives it a very wide field of vision.

Now think what sort of eyes a hawk needs. It has to be able to see a rat or mouse moving in the grass far below. So its eyes are close together on the front of its head. This allows the hawk to see in "stereo." The image sent from its left eye to its brain is very slightly different from that going from the right eye. This gives it much better information about the size and exact location of its prey.

What some animals lack in good eyesight they make up for with remarkable hearing. For example, insect-eating bats have very poor sight but they use echolocation to catch their food.

Some animals seem to have lost out on both good hearing and good eyesight. A bear, for example, will almost bump into you before it notices you're there. But then a bear has few enemies and does not need to chase its food. So it doesn't really need good eyesight or hearing in order to survive.

But how have human eyes and ears evolved, and how do they work? This book takes a close look at our senses of sight and hearing and explores the many ways in which they complement our life-styles. Problems and defects are discussed, as are the many different forms of treatment that exist.

LEFT With their excellent day and night vision, lions are well equipped to sneak up on grazing deer, wildebeests, and zebras.

RIGHT Just look at this serval cat's ears! If a tasty meal gets within range of those ears, it won't stand a chance.

TAKE A LOOK!

The colored part of the eye is called the iris, and the black dot that is in the middle is called the pupil.

Light enters your eye through the pupil. On a bright day the pupil gets smaller so that too much light cannot get in and damage the eye. In the dark, the pupil gets much bigger so it lets in as much light as possible.

There is a transparent membrane over the pupil. This is called the cornea. The cornea bends (focuses) light as it goes into the eye. Behind the pupil is the lens of the eye. This does the last bit of focusing before the light reaches the back of the eye where images are recorded on the retina.

Why do we need a cornea and a lens to focus light? Look at something a long way off. The rays of light coming into your eyes are lying alongside one another. Without a cornea or lens, they would go straight through your eye without ever coming together to produce an image of what you are looking at. You need your cornea and your lens to bend the rays of light inward so they meet precisely on your retina.

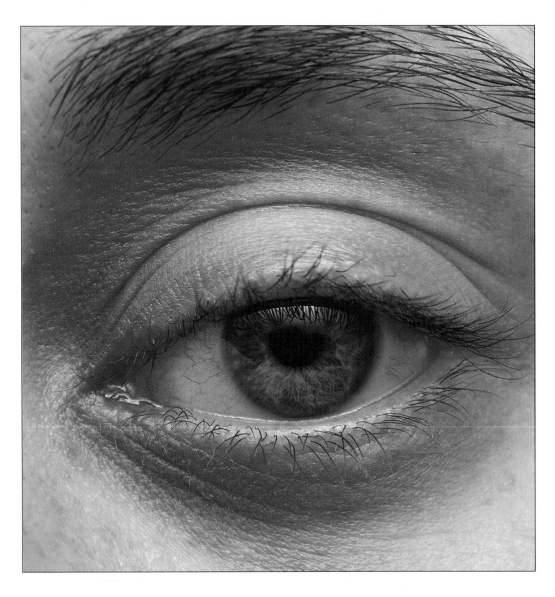

Doctors can find out a surprising amount about your health by looking into your eyes. For example, they can look through the pupil to the blood vessels at the back of the eye and see if you have high blood pressure.

6

Rays of light from objects enter the eye through the pupil. They are focused by the cornea and the lens, and an upside-down image falls on the retina. Messages travel to the brain along the optic nerve.

DIAGRAM OF AN EYE

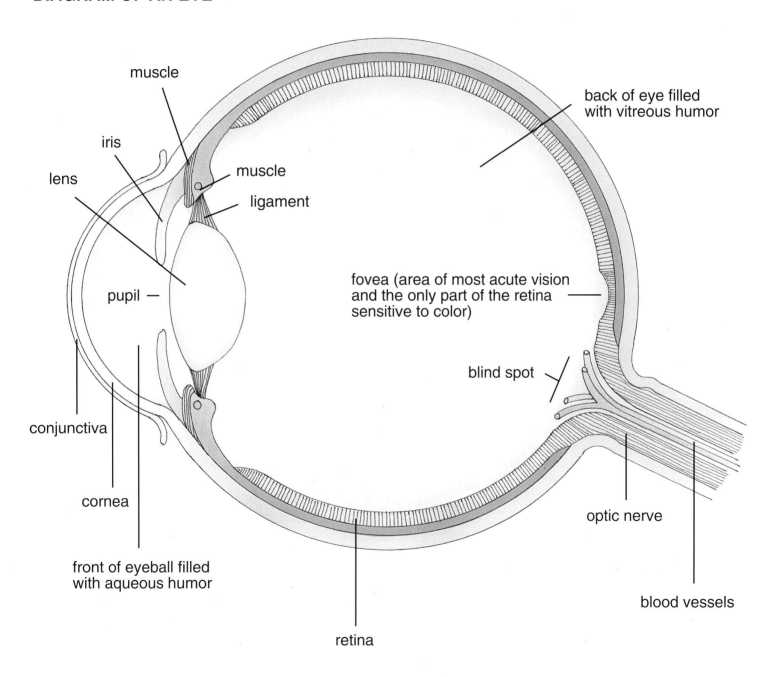

muscle

iris

lens

muscle

ligament

pupil —

conjunctiva

cornea

front of eyeball filled
with aqueous humor

back of eye filled
with vitreous humor

fovea (area of most acute vision
and the only part of the retina
sensitive to color)

blind spot

retina

optic nerve

blood vessels

Now look at something about 6 inches from your eyes. This time, the light rays coming from that object will be moving away from each other as they enter your eye. Again, without a cornea and a lens to bend them inward, there would be no chance of them meeting on your retina, so you wouldn't be able to see.

The way in which the cornea bends light is fixed. But muscles, attached to the lens by ligaments, can control how the light is focused after it has passed through the cornea. When you focus on a distant object, there is less need for fine-tuning, so the muscles remain relaxed. When they are relaxed, they pull the ligaments taut and the lens is pulled thin.

When you focus on something nearby, the lens needs to fine-tune the image. The muscles contract, so the ligaments become slack. This makes the elastic lens bulge and increases its focusing power.

INSECT VISION

Insects see quite differently from mammals. Some can do no more than distinguish light from dark. Others, such as this fruit fly, have thousands of light-focusing structures in their compound eyes. Each of these receives light from a small area and the image that the fly "sees" is an assortment of overlapping points. This kind of vision is not much good for recognizing things, but it is very good for detecting movement.

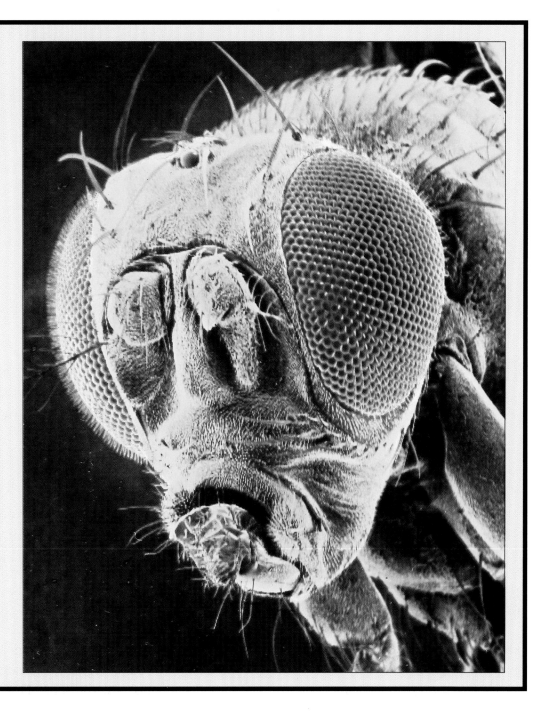

THE RETINA

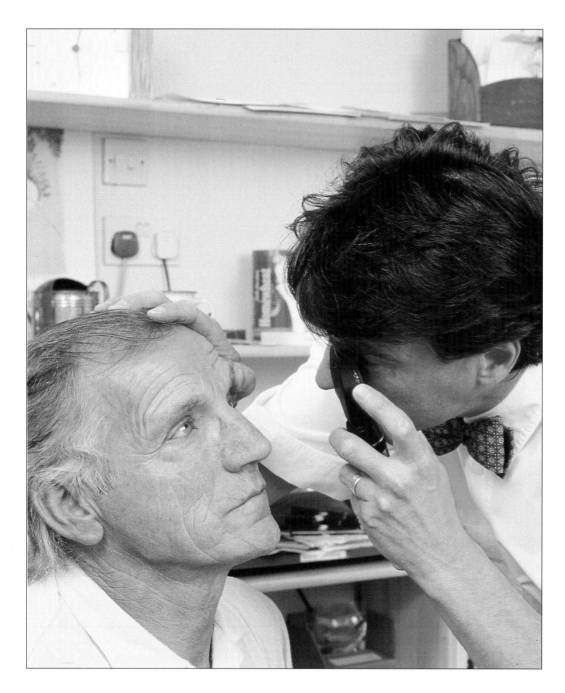

This doctor is using a device called an ophthalmoscope to see inside the patient's eye. The instrument directs a fine beam of light into the eye and contains magnifying lenses that allow the doctor to see the spot where the beam falls.

The image that lands on the retina after it has been focused by the cornea and the lens is upside down and back-to-front! Luckily for you, your brain can turn it around and make sense of it. In effect, the retina is like the film in a camera. It records what you are looking at, but the picture needs to be "developed," and made sense of, by the brain.

The retina contains millions of cells that are very sensitive to light. There are two types of these light-sensitive cells, and they do two main jobs. The first type are rods. Rods help you to see in the dark. The second type are cones. Cones allow you to see color.

Most light is focused on a part of the retina opposite the lens. This area is called the fovea.

The fovea consists exclusively of cones. Elsewhere the retina consists mostly of rods.

When they are stimulated by light, rods and cones send messages from the eye to the brain along the millions of neurons contained in the optic nerve. The point on the retina where the optic nerve leaves the eye has no rods or cones and is called the blind spot.

OPPOSITE These rods and cones have been magnified hundreds of times so that you can see them. Color has been added to distinguish the cones (blue) from the rods (pinkish purple).

NIGHT VISION

During World War II the British led the Germans to believe that Allied pilots had developed the ability to see in the dark by eating lots of carrots. In fact, they had radar. If you eat more carrots, you won't be able to see better at night. But carrots do contain vitamin A, which can be converted in the body to the pigment found in rods that enables you to see in the dark. So if you don't have enough vitamin A in your diet, you could find that you can't see very well at night.

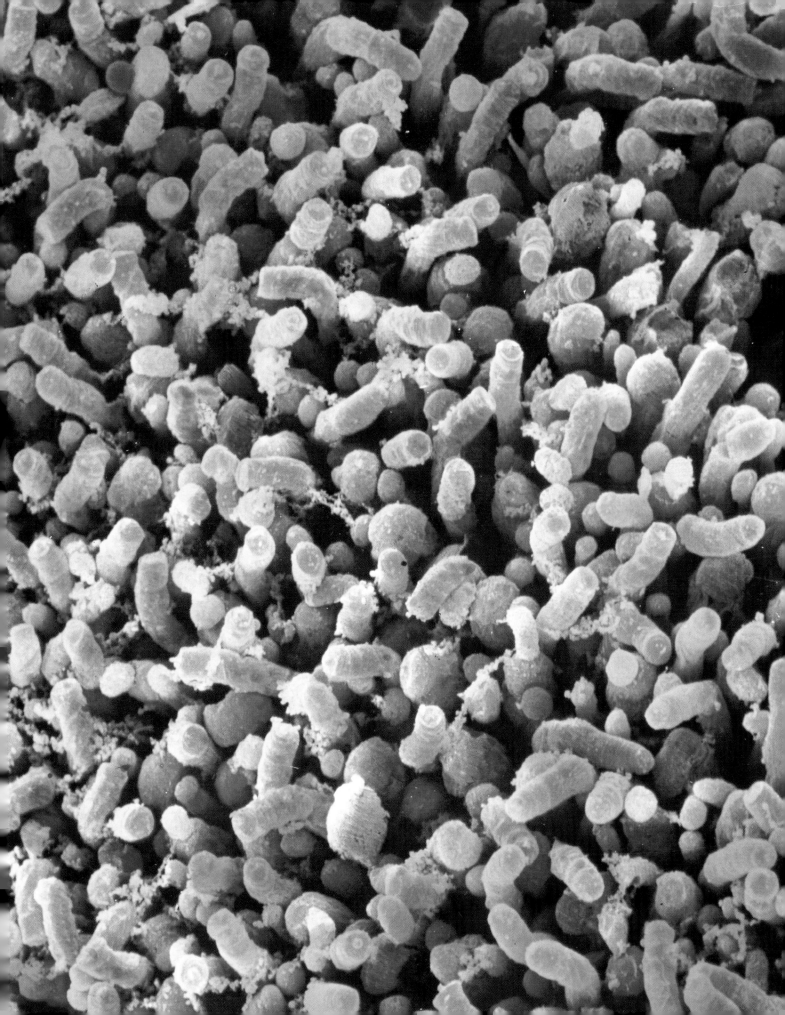

COLOR AND VISION

What is your favorite color? Is it a bright, happy color like yellow or orange? Or a strong, forceful color like red? Perhaps you prefer relaxing colors like pastel pinks or blues. Or maybe you like autumn shades of green and brown.

The colors you choose to wear or have around you say a lot about your personality and your mood. And, like it or not, other people will respond to the image you put forward. Appearances do count.

If you are always surrounded by dull, dark colors, people may think you are rather a depressed and negative sort of person. And if you always wear beiges and browns, you may appear mousy—wanting to blend in with the background instead of standing out from the rest of the crowd.

You don't have to be bright all the time. But you'll be surprised how much better you feel—and how differently people treat you—if you swap a bit of red for black or brown, light blue for navy, or yellow for sludgy greens.

Some people use color therapy to relieve stress and depression. This means using different colors to alter their moods. Pastel blues and greens are usually seen as colors to relax with, warm pinks and reds as colors for reassurance, and bold oranges and yellows are used as confidence boosters.

Some people express how good they feel about themselves with brightly colored clothes.

You're more likely to feel happier and calmer after a walk through a colorful park than along gray urban streets.

COLOR BLINDNESS

About one in twelve men have some degree of red-green color blindness. This means they lack either red or green cones and so have trouble making out shades of red and green. Color blindness is very rare in women.

What number can you see in the center of this picture? If you have normal vision, you'll see a 5. But if you are red-green color-blind you'll see a 2.

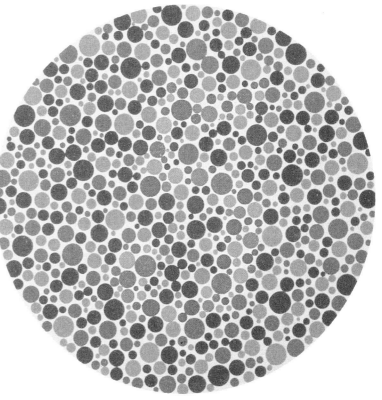

FIRST SIGHT

A baby can focus on its mother or father as soon as it is born. It can also see toys and other objects that are held in front of it. But it cannot follow a moving object with both eyes until it is two to three months old. In fact, young children have trouble focusing on something that is moving until they are two to three years old.

It is hard to be sure exactly how far very young children can see. Obviously, they cannot take a standard eye test, since they cannot read the letters on the chart. But investigations suggest that babies under one year can probably see only the equivalent of the top letter on a test chart. A year later, they can probably see

objects the same size as the fifth line. And by the time they are five, children can see normally.

In the first couple of years, many children appear to have a squint. One eye seems to turn inward more than the other. Early on, this is quite normal—the child is just finding it difficult to coordinate both eyes together. But if a squint goes on longer, it probably needs some kind of treatment.

Each year, several hundred children are born with very poor eyesight. Some can barely distinguish light from darkness. They cannot see their parents, brothers or sisters, toys, or even shapes. Because they cannot see, they do not

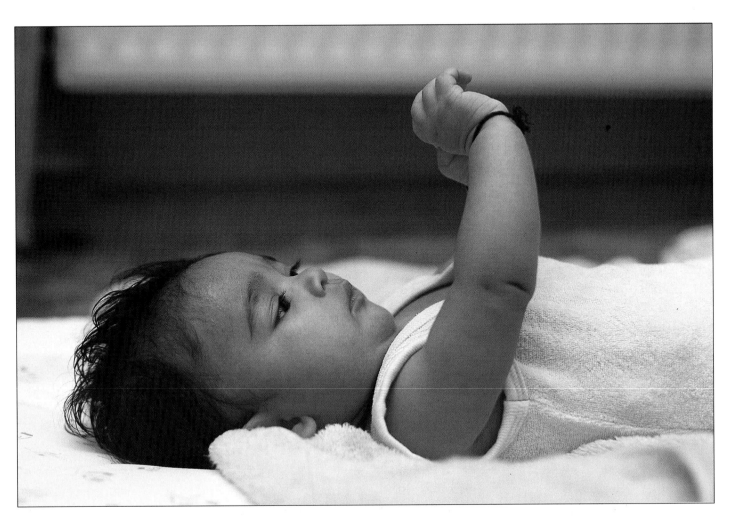

Soon this little girl will want to explore her surroundings.

14

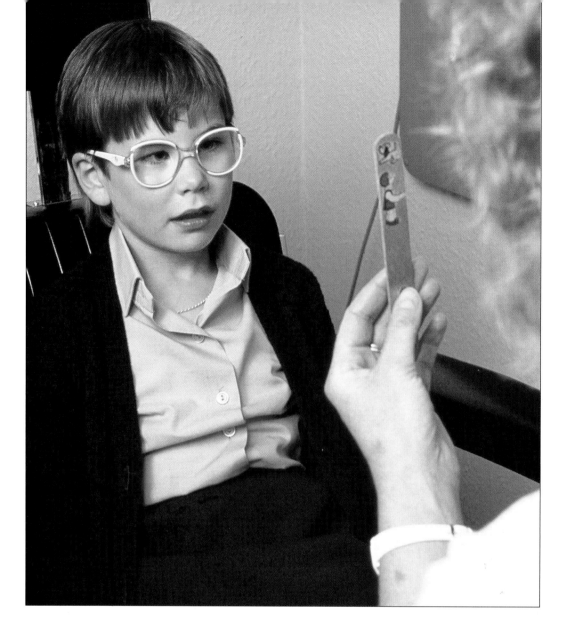

This child is having a squint test. First she looked at an object with one eye while her other eye was covered with a patch. When the patch was taken off, her newly uncovered eye had to move in order to focus on the object. That showed she has a squint.

react to things around them. They don't realize that they have hands and feet, so they don't reach out for things and explore. As time goes on, they become more and more unresponsive.

Recently, doctors have discovered that blind children and children who are partially sighted (have very poor sight) do much better if their problem is detected early. They can be shown that there is usually a solid object behind a noise, and they can learn how to explore their surroundings.

For example, a mother can put her blind son's hands on her mouth while she is talking so that he becomes aware of her movements and learns to use his hands to guide him toward the source of different sounds. Similarly, toys can be colored or illuminated so that partially sighted children have a better chance of seeing them. In this way, they can learn how to judge distance and follow moving objects.

SQUINTS

If you have a squint, only one of your eyes points at what you are looking at. The other eye points inward or outward. A true squint always needs treatment. It won't get better on its own and it is very hard to treat after eight or nine years of age. The brain only takes messages from the good eye, and the bad eye becomes weak and lazy. Glasses and eye exercises may cure the problem, or an operation may be necessary.

HAVING YOUR EYES TESTED

This girl is looking through a variety of lenses to see if the optician can improve her vision. When he finds the right lenses for her, she can have glasses made.

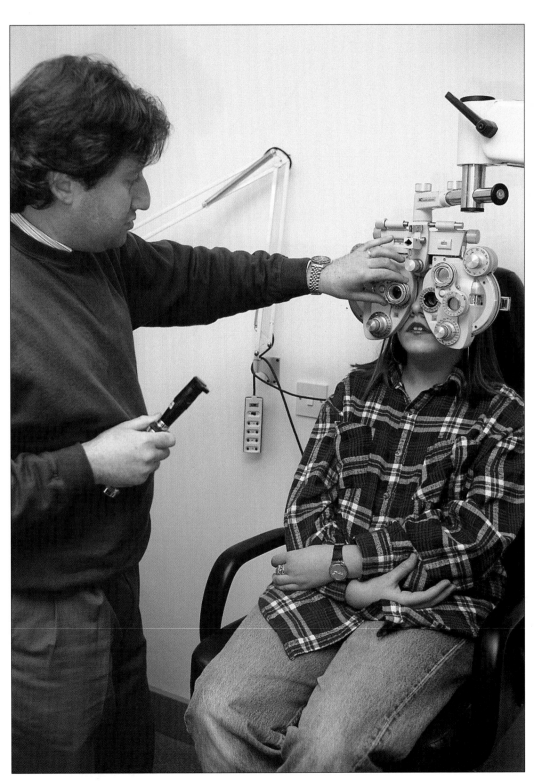

SENSITIVE EYES

Blue eyes are more sensitive to light than brown eyes, but only just. Slightly more people with blue eyes complain of discomfort in bright sunlight than brown-eyed people. This is because blue-eyed people have less protective pigment in the iris of the eye. Similarly, nearsighted people are more sensitive to bright light than farsighted people.

Perfect eyesight is called 20/20 vision. Have you got 20/20 vision? You cannot be sure unless you have had your eyes tested recently. We like to think that we have perfect eyesight, but few of us do.

When you have an eye test you will be asked to read letters on a chart 20 feet away. Since few opticians have rooms this long, you will usually be looking into a mirror 10 feet away, with the chart behind you. In effect, you are still looking at a chart 20 feet away because there is a distance of 10 feet between the letters and the mirror, and 10 feet from the mirror to you.

The letters on the chart get smaller and smaller. Normal (20/20) vision means that you can read all the letters on the chart. Someone who can read only the top, largest letter has 20/200 vision. This means that at 20 feet he or she can only read a letter that normal-sighted people can read at 200 feet.

Near vision is tested by reading a test card about 18 inches from your eyes.

The optician will also test your field of vision —what you can see out of the corner of your eye when you are looking straight ahead. This is especially important when people get older, because they may lose some of their field of vision.

You normally have an eye test when you start school. How often you are tested after this depends on the results of your first test. The more near- or farsighted you are, the more likely you are to need further checkups. If you notice that your vision is getting worse, you should definitely have a checkup. Don't suffer in silence. Tell someone!

NEAR- AND FARSIGHTEDNESS

Many people have difficulty focusing light rays onto the retina and so their vision is blurred.

People who are nearsighted cannot see distant objects clearly. The more nearsighted they are, the closer something must be for them to see it properly. Usually, nearsighted people have a longer than normal eyeball, so images fall short of the retina. This is called myopia. Myopic people need glasses or contact lenses to refocus distant images on to the retina.

Farsighted people have a shorter than normal eyeball, so images are focused behind the retina. This is called hypermetropia. However, up to the age of about forty, the lens can adapt to refocus images onto the retina so they can see normally without glasses or contact lenses. But because the muscles in our eyes weaken as we get older, farsighted people find that eventually they can no longer focus properly and need glasses to see close up. How close can you hold a book and still read the words clearly? Children and farsighted adults can hold a book less than 4 inches from their eyes and still focus the words. But the lens hardens as we get older and the muscles that make it get wider or thinner get weaker. This makes it harder to focus and many people need glasses for reading or close work. This impairment is called presbyopia.

ASTIGMATISM

Some people are born with an abnormally shaped cornea or lens. It doesn't curve evenly, so they focus light rays from some directions better than others. Luckily they can wear glasses with lenses that will even out their own lens so that they can see normally.

Nearsightedness (myopia)

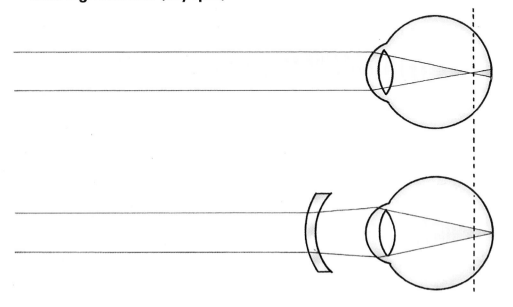

Objects close to the eye can be focused properly, but the point of focus for distant objects is in front of the retina.

Nearsightedness is corrected by a diverging lens.

Farsightedness (hypermetropia)

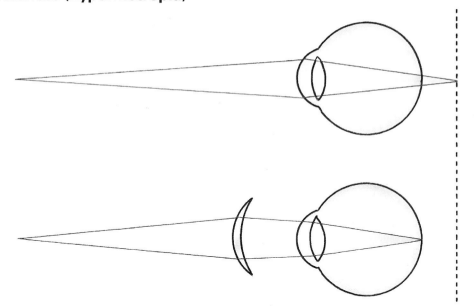

Distant objects can be focused properly, but the point of focus for an object close to the eye is behind the retina.

Farsightedness is corrected by a converging lens.

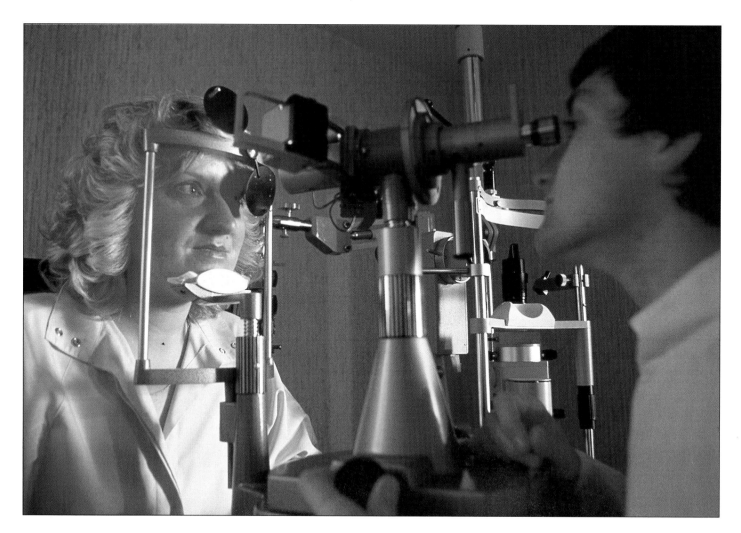

This optician is using a machine called a keratometer to measure the curvature of the woman's cornea. This will tell him if she has astigmatism.

CONTACT LENSES

Many people choose to wear contact lenses instead of glasses to correct problems with their eyesight. Most people feel they look better wearing lenses rather than glasses. Other people cannot tell when someone is wearing contact lenses, and wearers don't have to keep putting them on and taking them off. They don't pinch the bridge of your nose, press against your face, or steam up when you get hot. You can also play sports in them.

But contact lenses can take a bit of getting used to. They are not practical for everybody. Some people find them too uncomfortable to keep in their eyes. Others can leave them in for only a few hours at a time.

The two most popular types of contact lens are hard lenses and soft lenses. Hard lenses are small, firm plastic disks. They rest on the cornea of the eye. They are cheap and long-lasting, but some people find them uncomfortable and it takes a while for the eyes to get used to them. So you have to build up gradually the amount of time you leave them in. Hard lenses must be taken out at night and kept very clean. The eyes can become dry and particles of dust and dirt can get under the lenses.

Soft lenses are made of a watery gel and they are so light and flexible that people soon forget they've got them in. But vision isn't quite so sharp as with hard lenses and more time has to

It takes patience, but most people soon learn to use contact lenses.

Disposable lenses are soft lenses that have been designed to be worn overnight like extended wear lenses, but are thrown away after seven days. This reduces the risk of infection.

At present, manufacturers are working on soft lenses that can be worn for twenty-four hours and then thrown away. However, they are likely to be very expensive.

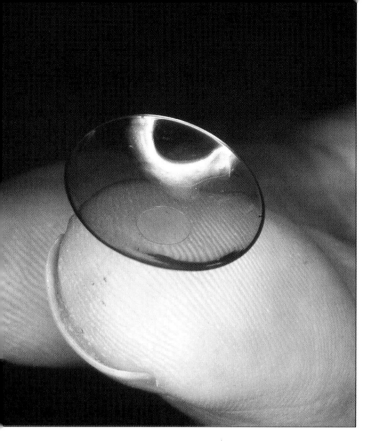

ABOVE Nowadays, you can even change the color of your eyes! All you need is enough money to buy a pair of tinted contact lenses.

be spent cleaning and disinfecting soft lenses. They also tear more easily and don't last as long. Newer types of lenses include gas-permeable, extended wear (can be left in the eyes for a long time), and, most recently, disposable lenses.

Gas-permeable lenses are a cross between hard and soft lenses. They allow some oxygen to pass through them. This means that your eyes don't get dry and uncomfortable, as they might do with other kinds of contact lenses.

Extended wear lenses were designed to be kept in all day and all night and cleaned every few weeks. They are very thin and soft, but people who wear them are more likely to get eye infections.

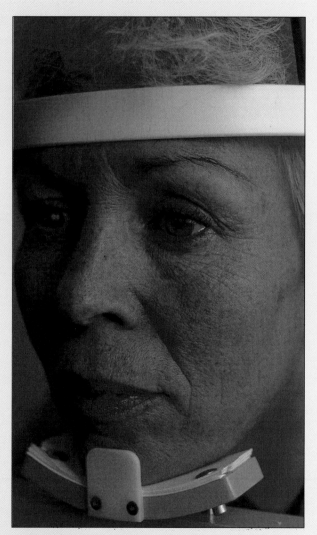

LASER POWER

A growing number of near- and farsighted people are throwing away their glasses and contact lenses and having their eyeballs reshaped by laser surgery (above) to improve their eyesight. Some opticians and specialists are worried about the long-term effects of laser surgery, but many people are very pleased with the results.

LOOKING AFTER YOUR EYES

Put a light on. You'll strain your eyes!
Don't sit so close to the television. You'll damage your eyes!
If you play with that computer game all day, you'll ruin your eyes!

How many times have people said these things to you? Well, they are wrong! If you need glasses and you don't wear them, you may tire your eyes and give yourself a headache. Also you will not see as well as you should. But there will be no permanent damage.

Reading without enough light can make your eyes hurt and give you a headache, too. But it will not cause lasting damage. Nor will watching television or a computer screen for long periods —although a flickering screen may give you a headache and make you feel sick!

You cannot damage your eyes by using them "too much." You can only improve your sight with glasses, contact lenses, or, if necessary, with

Spending all day in front of a computer screen may tire your eyes and give you a headache.

Always wear protective glasses when you are advised to. You can't get a new pair of eyes.

surgery. Eye exercises will only help eyesight if you have a squint. They will not help you to see better if you are far- or nearsighted.

All this doesn't mean you can abuse your eyes. After all, you only get one pair! Looking into a very bright light can damage the retina. Watching the sun through binoculars or a telescope can burn the inside of your eyes. Don't do it!

Wear sunglasses to protect your eyes if you are walking about in bright sunlight. Always wear protective glasses if you are using chemicals or machines that could damage your eyes. It is also a good idea to wear eye protection when playing games such as tennis.

FIRST AID FOR EYES

If a bit of dust or grit gets into your eye, try "blinking" it out or washing it out with water. If this doesn't work, see a doctor. Similarly, if you get a chemical in your eye, wash it out with lots of water right away and get medical help.

Don't let a small child play with pointed objects because they can so easily penetrate an eye and cause permanent damage. And if you have a problem with your eyes—pain, redness, swelling, or discharge—always go to a doctor. Don't wait for the problem to get worse.

DIABETIC EYES

Diabetics have to control their blood sugar levels. This is not only to prevent them from feeling ill, but also to protect their eyes.

Most diabetics have some problems with their vision when the disease is first spotted, but these usually disappear once their diabetes is treated with insulin or other glucose-lowering drugs. If diabetics don't control the amount of sugar in their blood, the blood vessels in the retina may bleed and lead to gradual loss of sight.

All diabetics should have regular eye checks, even if they keep their blood sugar under control. Doctors can look at the retina for any early signs of damage. Any problems can be treated with a laser.

In addition to using medicine, diabetics can learn to control their blood sugar levels by watching what they eat and avoiding being overweight. It is very important for people with diabetes to take their illness seriously.

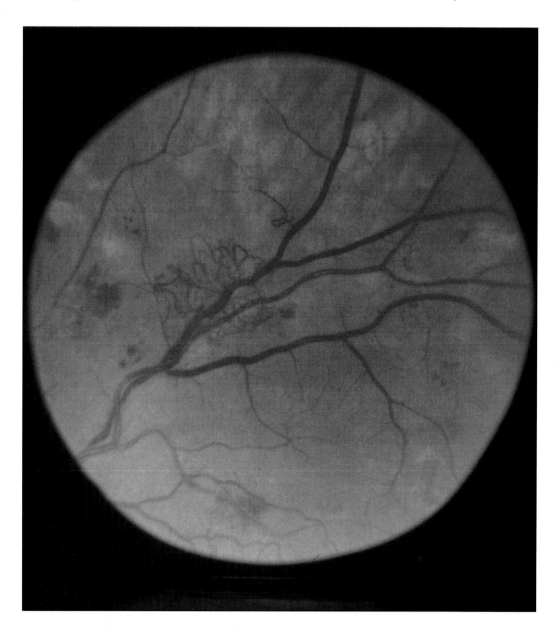

This is a photograph of a diabetic's retina. The fine red lines, just left of center, are a symptom of the disease.

Candy can quickly increase a diabetic's blood sugar to dangerous levels. If she eats them often, she could damage her eyes.

WATCH WHAT YOU EAT

- Eat less fat.
- Eat about 1 pound of fruit and vegetables a day.
- Don't have more than 1 ounce of sugar in your low fat/high fiber diet each day.
- Don't have more than a teaspoonful of salt in your food each day.
- Don't eat too much protein.

TUNNEL VISION

Imagine what it would be like if you could only see straight ahead of you, as if you were looking through a long tube. You would miss out on just about everything that was happening on either side of you.

This is what happens to people who have an eye disease called glaucoma (tunnel vision). Usually it creeps up on middle-aged and elderly people without them realizing it. The disease is not unheard of in young people.

Once part of the field of vision has been lost, it cannot be restored. But if glaucoma is found at any early stage, it can be treated so that it doesn't get any worse.

Glaucoma results from a buildup of pressure in the eye. Normally the eye has a very effective drainage system that gets rid of excess fluid. But in glaucoma this seems to go wrong. When the pressure in the eye gets too high, it interferes with the blood supply to the retina and the optic nerve, leaving them short of oxygen and nutrients. It is this that leads to the loss of vision.

If the rise in pressure is found early enough, people can use drops to reduce the pressure in the eyes and halt the loss of vision. Sometimes an operation is needed to improve drainage in the eyes so that the pressure falls.

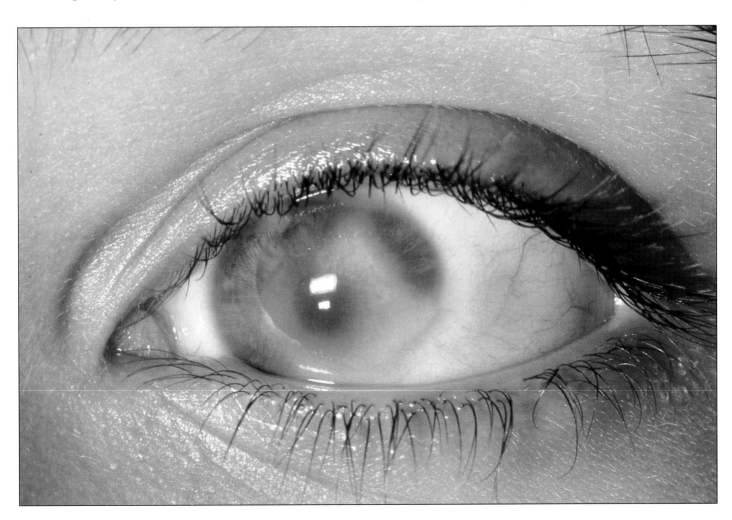

This girl was born with glaucoma. Normally, sufferers develop the disease when they are older.

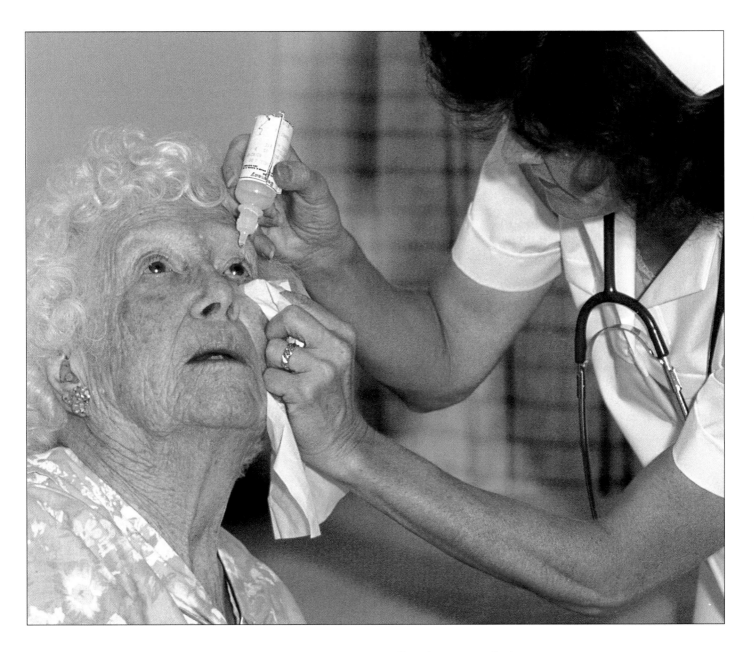

BE ON THE LOOKOUT

Eyedrops can help prevent glaucoma from getting any worse, but they cannot cure it.

Glaucoma affects about 1 in 100 people over the age of forty and it tends to run in families. Someone who has a close relative with the disease is ten times more likely to get it than someone who hasn't. This is why it is important for relatives of someone with glaucoma to have the pressure in their eyes checked regularly— every five years when they are under forty and every two years when they are over forty.

CATARACTS

Have you ever looked into someone's eyes and noticed that the middle part is all cloudy? They have cataracts. This means that the protein in the lens of the eye has changed—a bit like the way an egg white goes from clear to solid when it is beaten.

When a lens gets cloudy, light rays cannot get through properly and the person may gradually go blind. Most people with cataracts are elderly. In fact, nearly all people over sixty-five have some cloudiness in their lenses, but only a few get so bad that they cannot see at all.

Until about ten years ago you could tell when people had been treated for cataracts because they wore glasses with very thick lenses. This was because their own cloudy lenses had been removed, so they needed the strongest possible glasses to enable them to focus. Even then, the result wasn't very good. Often, they couldn't see very well and when they took off their glasses, they couldn't focus at all.

Since cataract treatment did not work very well, people waited until their own lenses had clouded over completely before having the operation. Surgery was a last resort.

Today all this has changed. Surgery is much more effective because the old, cloudy lenses can be replaced with new, plastic lenses some-

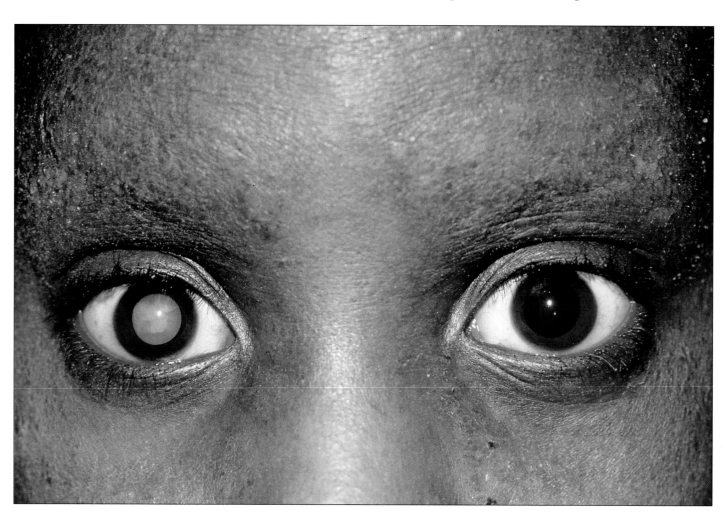

This cataract can be removed safely and replaced with a new lens.

what like contact lenses. These are inserted in the eyes, and the person may not need glasses at all. The operation isn't the answer for everyone. But it is helping many elderly people to see who ten years ago would have had to live with very poor eyesight.

NEW CORNEAS FOR OLD

The lens isn't the only part of the eye that can be replaced. People whose corneas have been damaged by injury or infection can also be given new ones. But this operation requires donated human corneas.

Corneas are one of the items listed on organ donor cards and they can give sight to people who would otherwise be blind. Doctors can now freeze-dry corneal tissue and reshape it, so they can use more donated corneas than ever before. Make sure you carry an organ donor card.

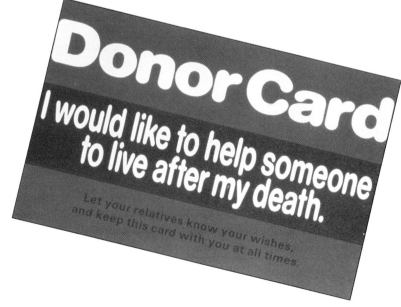

Donor Card
I would like to help someone to live after my death.
Let your relatives know your wishes, and keep this card with you at all times.

ABOVE Help someone else to see. Carry an organ donor card.

VISUAL AIDS

Many blind people can work as keyboard operators thanks to specially adapted computers. This computer can translate 128 different characters, including all the letters of the alphabet and numbers, into a language that other computers understand.

Cathy sits down at her portable computer. She switches it on and reaches for the screen. She feels the words she is keying into her computer on the rows of tiny holes and pins that make up the Braille display.

Cathy can touch type a QWERTY keyboard so she doesn't need the special Braille keyboard that is also available. When she has finished her report, Cathy decides to hear the whole thing through and switches on the voice simulator. It reads her report.

This isn't science fiction. Computers like this have already been made and are being improved all the time. With the help of such machines, blind people can do jobs that would have been out of the question just a few years ago. Sitting in an office surrounded by the latest computers, they can communicate with clients who need never know they are blind.

At home, too, life has been made much easier. Many household machines can be worked by remote controls, and thousands of books are now available on tape or in Braille.

FLYING EYE

Thousands of people in developing countries have had their sight restored and many more have had serious eye disorders treated with the help of Project Orbis. This is the Flying Eye service, which is getting to some of the remote parts of the world where there are no doctors or medical supplies.

A team of eye surgeons arrives with all the modern equipment needed to treat conditions like cataracts, diabetic eye disease, and corneal infections. News travels fast and people come from far and wide to have their eyes treated. Then it's up and away for the medical team as they fly off to the next place in need of their help.

INSIDE THE HUMAN EAR

What you can see of your ear is the least interesting part! Go beyond the outer flaps and the narrow waxy passages, and eventually you will come to one of the most remarkable parts of the human body.

First there's the eardrum—a membrane like the surface of a drum that makes sound waves vibrate. It's stretched across a narrow opening into the middle ear. In the middle ear there are three moving bones that send the vibrating sound waves across to another membrane and into the inner ear.

In the inner ear is a coiled tube that looks something like a snail. It's called the cochlea. The cochlea is divided into three fluid-filled canals separated by membranes. The membrane

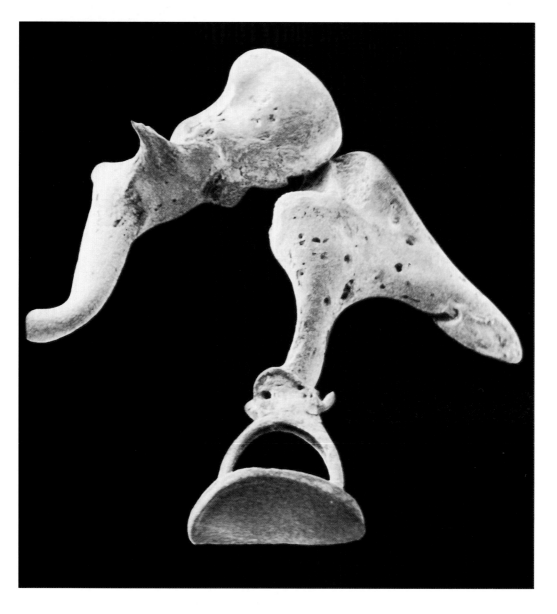

These are the three bones in the middle ear. Sound is conducted across the malleus (top left) to the incus (to the right) and on to the stapes (bottom), which in turn conducts sound to the inner ear.

that separates the second and third canals is called the basilar membrane. It is lined with thousands of sensitive hair cells, which are connected to the brain by nerves. The nerves are like the filling in a sandwich, with the basilar membrane below and a second membrane, the tectorial membrane, above.

As sound waves pass through the cochlea, the fluid in the canals moves around. This, in turn, sends ripples through the hair cells, making them rub against the tectorial membrane. This excites the hair cells so they send messages along the auditory nerve to the brain. Some hair cells send messages when they are disturbed by high-pitched sounds, like whistles. Others react to low-frequency noises, like foghorns.

This diagram shows the structure of the human ear in cross-section. The middle and inner ear are drawn on a larger scale than the outer ear.

DIAGRAM OF AN EAR

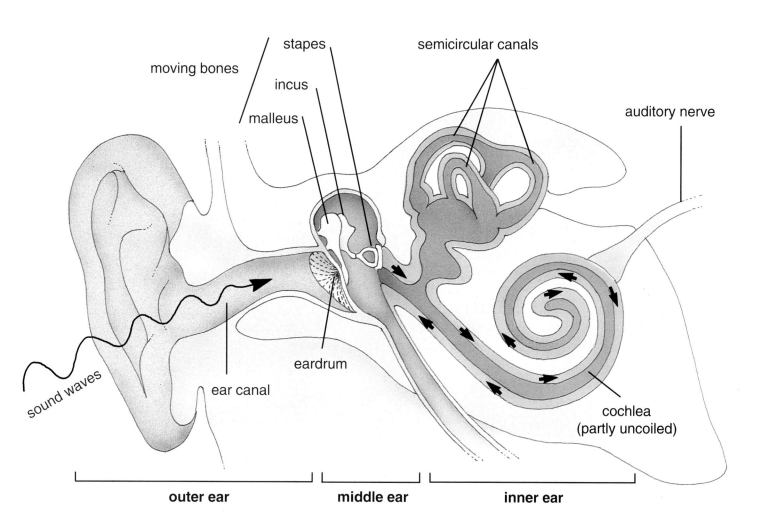

moving bones

stapes

incus

malleus

semicircular canals

auditory nerve

eardrum

ear canal

sound waves

cochlea (partly uncoiled)

outer ear　　　　middle ear　　　　inner ear

BALANCE

The ear contains one other important piece of equipment—the balance mechanism. This also consists of canals—three semicircular ones at right angles to each other. They, too, contain fluid and hair cells. When you move your head, the hair cells (above) move and send messages to the brain about what you have done so that you can keep your balance.

EAR INFECTIONS

Most of the pupils in your class will have had an ear infection at some time in their lives. Many will have suffered frequent bouts of infection throughout their childhoods.

Nearly half of all three-year-olds get an ear infection in any given year. It is the most common cause of hearing loss in children and thousands have operations to try to sort out the problem.

The middle ear becomes swollen and painful as infected fluid builds up behind the eardrum.

The infection can be treated with antibiotics to kill the bacteria that are causing it and about half of cases clear up within a couple of months. The problem is that these infections can come back again and again.

Hearing tests show that those who suffer from ear infections hear less than other children. They are always saying "What?" or "Pardon?" or they just don't respond when you speak to them. It's a bit like trying to hear when you've got cotton wool in your ears.

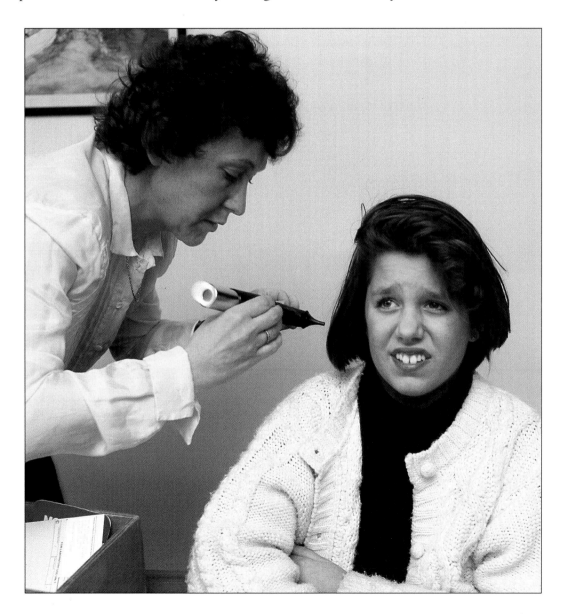

This girl is about to have the wax taken out of her ears to try to help improve her hearing.

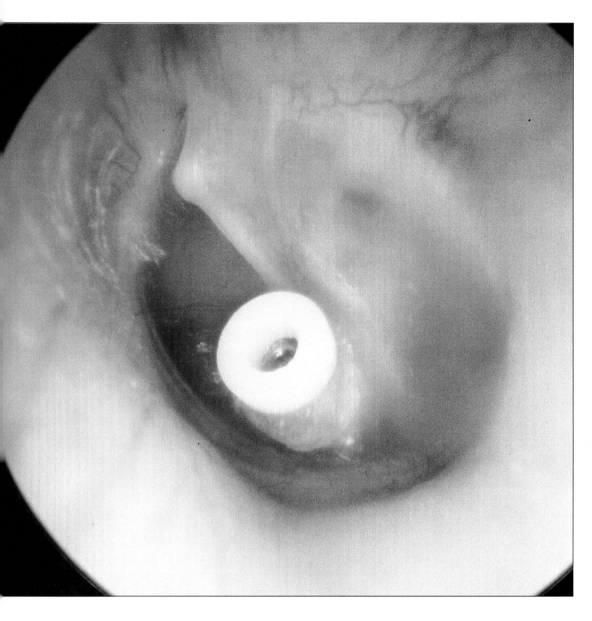

This grommet has been inserted into a child's ear to improve drainage and prevent him from getting infections. Some children need several sets of grommets before they finally stop suffering from ear infections.

Children do eventually grow out of the ear infections. They clear up and the children can hear properly again. But by this time they may have gotten behind in their schoolwork and find it hard to catch up. This is why parents, teachers, and doctors have become so interested in ear infections and why so many children are having operations. A few have their adenoids removed, but usually a small tube called a grommet is inserted into the eardrum to drain the infected fluid from the middle ear. There is a lot of debate about whether or not this is worthwhile. Children have to go into the hospital, many get infections after the grommets have been put in, and the improvement in their hearing wears off quite quickly. More and more people are starting to wonder if it's worth it.

SURGICAL FASHIONS

In the 1950s and 1960s, few children went through childhood without having their tonsils and/or their adenoids out. Today, the operations are much less common and children are far more likely to have grommet surgery instead.

Childhood illnesses haven't changed, but the fashions for treatment have. Who knows what will be in fashion in the year 2010?

DEAF, NOT DAFT

About 21 million people in the U.S. have lost some or all of their hearing. Some were born deaf, while others have lost their hearing as a result of an accident or illness. One thing is sure: Being deaf does not mean you can't think. So never treat deaf people as though they are stupid. Instead, try to find out how they communicate.

Most elderly people have lost some of their hearing and about one in three over the age of seventy needs a hearing aid.

These deaf children go to an ordinary elementary school and have no trouble communicating with their friends. They use lipreading and sign language.

Listening to loud music can damage your hearing. Don't do it!

Deafness takes many forms. One ear may be worse than the other. Some people find it hard to hear high-pitched noises, while others lose the ability to hear deep, low-pitched sounds. Some have hearing loss at all frequencies. Gradually, a sound needs to be louder and louder for them to hear it.

Many people can hear you if you talk to them in a quiet room but have trouble when there is a lot of background noise—music, for example, or other people talking.

Some people suffer from a condition called tinnitus. Not only can they not hear properly, but they also have a frequent if not constant ringing in their ears. Tinnitus is difficult to treat and can be very distressing.

One of the most common reasons why people lose their hearing is that they have damaged it by listening to very loud noises. You've probably seen people using pneumatic drills on the roads without any protective earmuffs. They are crazy!

Just think what they are doing to all the delicate hair cells in their cochleas. The first cells to die are those that respond to high frequencies. Then the others die, too.

You can also damage your hearing if you listen to music that is too loud. No one yet knows how much damage the personal stereo revolution is doing to the nation's hearing, so it's probably best to keep the volume down.

HEARING TESTS

All babies are given a simple test. A rattle is shaken behind their heads or a loud noise is made behind them to see if they will turn around. Hearing tests for older children and adults are much more complex. It is possible to find out exactly which frequencies can be heard and which can't.

This five-year-old girl has to say "yes" every time she hears a sound.

LEARNING TO SPEAK

Do you know when you started to talk? Babies start to babble and make noises when they are only three to six months old. But most are around two years of age before they use recognizable words. This is about the time when the nerves in the brain that deal with language get the fatty coating they need to work properly.

By the time they are three, most children have mastered how to coordinate their tongue and lip movements with their breathing, so that they can speak. Over the next few years they learn more words and can make sentences.

But children need to be able to hear others speak in order to speak themselves. It seems that if they don't learn to speak by the time they reach puberty, they never fully catch up. People who are born deaf need extra help. If you have never heard any sounds, it is hard to understand how to make them.

Deaf children have to see the effect that sound has and then try to copy it. Some letters are easier to "see" than others. Hold a piece of paper close to your mouth and say the letter "b" as you would to say "ball." You can see and feel the vibration that the sound waves make as they come out of your mouth and hit the piece of paper. Other letters are much harder to learn because you can't "see" the effect they make. Hold the paper up again and say "a" as in "apple." There is no obvious effect.

This little boy was born deaf, but he is being taught how to speak.

Luckily, there are special machines that show what different sound waves look like on a screen. Deaf children can copy the facial movements that their teacher makes to produce the sounds they see on the screen. But it is a slow process, especially for someone who has been deaf from birth.

People who lose their hearing after they have learned to speak have fewer problems, especially if they lose their hearing in later life. They may speak rather loudly or too softly because they cannot hear themselves, and they tend to interrupt when they aren't aware that others are talking. But their voices will not change much.

SPEECH THERAPY

Speech therapists can help people who have trouble with their speech. They don't just help deaf people; they can also help people who have other nerve damage that makes it difficult for them to speak properly—such as after a stroke.

BETTER HEARING

These deaf people are learning to communicate better at a sign and song workshop. Some people find sign language easier to use than others.

Modern hearing aids are so small that you can hardly see them. They're quite different from the huge ear trumpets that people used in earlier centuries. Even so, only a small number of people who need a hearing aid actually wear one regularly. Some people don't like to admit they have a problem with their hearing. They are afraid that if others know they are losing their hearing, they will assume they are losing their minds as well.

A hearing aid does take some getting used to. If it is switched on too high, the person may just get a lot of feedback and interference. Everyone has a different pattern of hearing loss. Some people have more trouble with high-frequency sounds, others with sounds at low frequency. Each hearing aid needs to be adapted to the individual's needs.

Some of the more advanced hearing aids can be programmed to adapt to a person's surroundings. For example, if you are in a crowded restaurant, you want your hearing aid to tune in to the conversation at your table, not to that at the next table or to dishes breaking in the kitchen! Or, if you are going for a quiet walk in the country, you want your hearing aid to pick up all the sounds around you, not just those nearby. The newer aids can do this, but, unfortunately, they tend to be more expensive than standard hearing aids.

Most modern hearing aids are so small that they fit snugly behind or inside the wearer's ear. In the past (left) they were bigger and much more noticeable.

Most people with poor hearing become good at lipreading what people are saying to them and some learn sign language. In the home, some household appliances can be fitted with flashing lights to show when they need to be switched on or off. Doorbells and telephones can have similar devices fitted. Specially trained "hearing dogs" respond to sounds and alert their deaf owners.

NEW EARS FOR OLD

A growing number of severely deaf people are having implants in their cochleas to give them some hearing. A microphone/sound processing box (which looks rather like a personal stereo) picks up sounds and sends them to a transmitter/receiver under the skin behind the ear. This in turn triggers the implant in the cochlea, which stimulates the auditory nerve. This means that the hair cells that normally register sounds are bypassed. Results vary, but on the whole they are good. People with some hearing find they need to do less lipreading. Those with no hearing are at least aware of changing sounds around them.

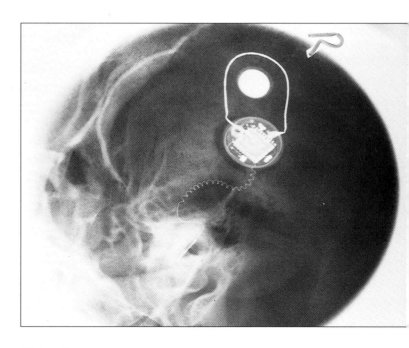

This electronic ear implant can improve hearing, though it cannot take the place of the human ear.

SUPERSENSE

Imagine you could see like a hawk and hear like a bat! It might not be as useful as you think. True, if you had a hawk's eyesight, you could see small moving objects from a great distance. But if you had a bat's hearing, you'd be constantly plagued by high-pitched screams and whistles.

Future research is unlikely to try to improve on what nature has given us. Instead, it will try to improve the outlook for people whose sight and hearing have failed them.

Cochlea implants are already improving life for some deaf people and recent studies have shown it may be possible to grow cochlea hair cells in the laboratory and transplant them into the inner ear. Exciting advances are also being made in eye surgery and the first transplants of retinal cells have already been performed successfully.

A lot of work is still needed to perfect these new techniques. The nerve pathways that allow us to see and hear are among the most complicated in the body. Mimicking them is proving a mammoth task and we will be well into the twenty-first century before doctors can offer people with sight and hearing problems any real alternatives to current treatments.

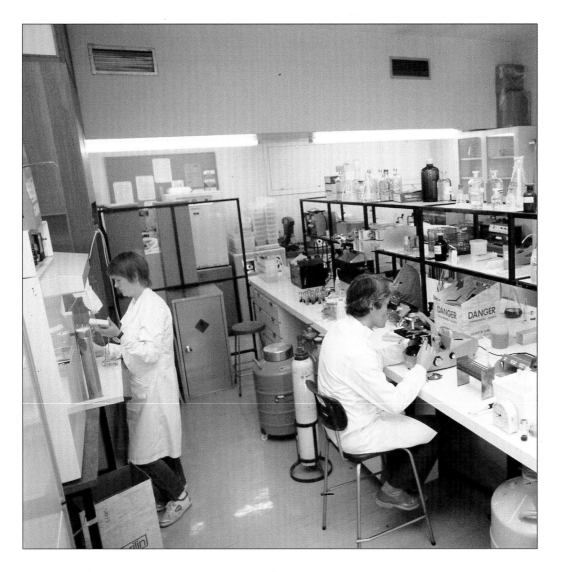

LEFT Researchers continually work to develop better hearing aids that can be adapted to individual needs.

RIGHT The complex patterns on the computer screen represent the single word "baby." Computers are being developed that can recognize the sounds needed to make different words. It's possible that soon we will be able to talk to our machines.

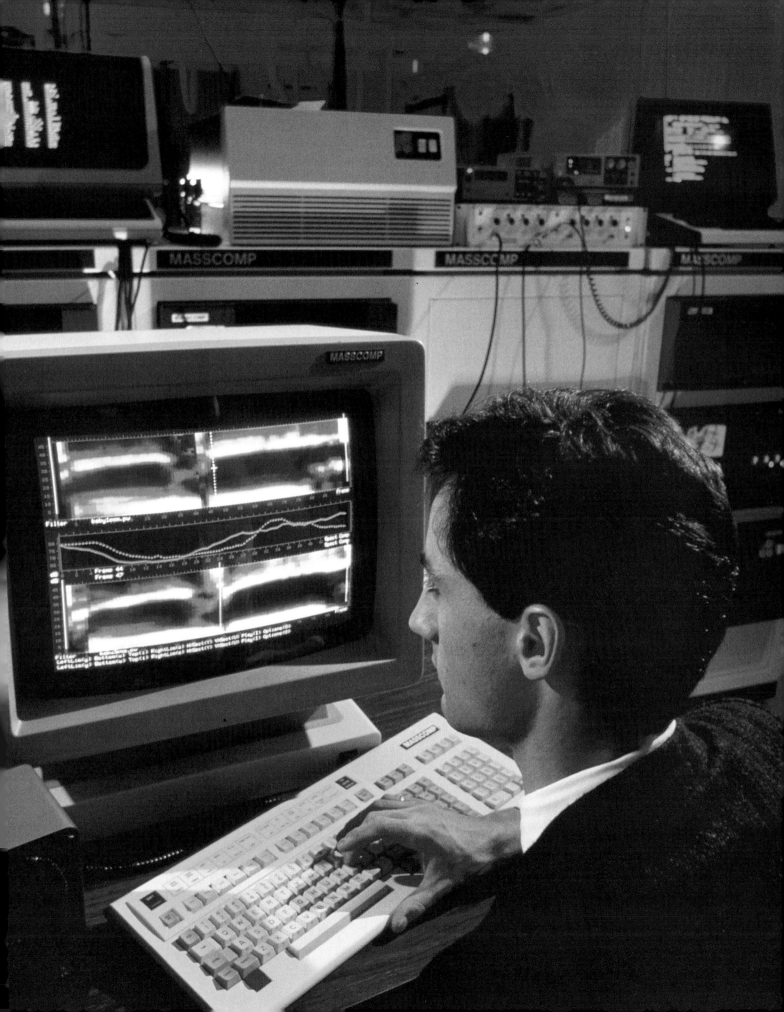

GLOSSARY

adenoids glandlike tissues in the nose that may become swollen in both children and adults and block the airway.

astigmatism visual problem caused by unevenly shaped eyeball.

cataract thickening of the lens of the eye that makes the eye look cloudy and can lead to blindness.

cochlea snail-shaped structure in the inner ear where the cells that pick up sound are found.

cone retinal cell in the eye that picks up color.

cornea transparent membrane over the pupil. It bends light rays entering the eye.

diabetes hormone abnormality that results in too much sugar in the blood.

eardrum membrane that carries sound vibration from the outer to the middle ear.

echolocation a system involving echoes that is used by bats to find their prey.

frequency the number of sound waves that reach an object in a second.

glaucoma tunnel vision resulting from raised pressure of fluid in the eye.

hypermetropia farsightedness.

iris colored part of the eye.

laser powerful beam of light used to treat eye diseases.

lens jellylike disk that focuses light entering the eye.

myopia nearsightedness.

neuron nerve cell.

presbyopia sight change that results from wear and tear of the lens and eye muscles and usually occurs with age.

pupil opening in the center of the eye where light gets in.

retina back of the eye, where images are recorded.

rods cells in the retina that enable people to see in dim light.

squint eye problem in which one eye looks in a different direction from the other.

tonsils glandlike tissue in the throat that can become swollen and painful.

wavelength distance between the crest of two waves of light or two waves of sound.

FURTHER READING

Cash, Terry. *Sound.* New York: Franklin Watts, 1989.

Darling, David. *Sounds Interesting: The Science of Acoustics.* New York: Dillon Press, 1991.

Gardner, Robert. *Experimenting with Sound.* New York: Franklin Watts, 1991.

Lampton, Christopher. *Sound: More Than What You Hear.* Hillside, New Jersey: Enslow Publishers, 1992.

Parker, Steve. *The Eye and Seeing.* New York: Franklin Watts, 1989.

Samz, Jane. *Vision.* New York: Chelsea House, 1990.

Ward, Brian. *The Eye and Sight.* New York: Franklin Watts, 1981.

ACKNOWLEDGMENTS

Chapel Studios 25 (top); National Medical Slide Bank 29; Oxford Scientific 4 (Rafi Ben-Shahar), 5 (Steve Turner); Panos Pictures 31 (Jeremy Hartley); Reflections cover/title page; Sally & Richard Greenhill 14, 16, 35, 37, 38, 39, 40, 42; Skjold 13 (top), 17; Science Photo Library 6 (Martin Dohrn), 8 (CNRI), 9 (Simon Fraser), 11 (P. Motta), 13 (bottom, Adam Hart-Davies), 15 (Adam Hart-Davies), 19 (A. McClenaghan), 21 (bottom, Will & Deni McIntyre), 22 (Robert Isear), 23 (John Howard), 24 (Western Ophthalmic Hospital), 26 (Dr. P. Marazzi), 27 (D. Campions), 28 (Western Ophthalmic Hospital), 29 (bottom, C. Priest), 30 (Adam Hart-Davies), 32 (CNRI), 34 (P. Motta), 36 (Tony Wright), 41 (Hattie Young), 45 (Hank Morgan); St. Mary's Hospital 43 (bottom); Tony Stone Worldwide 12 (Peter Correz); Topham 10, 44; Wayland Picture Library 20, 25 (bottom), 43 (top); Western Ophthalmic Hospital 21 (top).
Artwork by Malcolm S. Walker.

INDEX